2 English Short Stories

—

Easy to read

2 English Short Stories

Easy to read

New Crime Stories

For all ages

Irmgard Hetterich

**Bibliografische Information der
Deutschen Nationalbibliothek**
Die Deutsche Nationalbibliothek verzeichnet diese
Publikation in der Deutschen Nationalbibliografie;
detaillierte bibliografische Daten sind im Internet über
http://dnb.d-nb.de abrufbar.

@ 2014 Irmgard Hetterich
Herstellung und Verlag:
Books on Demand GmbH
Norderstedt

ISBN: 978-3-7357-9109-2

Inhaltsverzeichnis

A Deadly Error.. 9

Theft at Dawn 27

A Deadly Error

Bob woke up as usual with the sound of the seven o'clock train whooshing by. But this day won't be like all the others, where he bravely goes to work at eight o'clock in the morning. No, he's got a plan. Today he will drive to the next town and rob the bank. He could already anticipate the newspaper headlines for tomorrow: "Bank robbery". "City Bank robbed." No trace of thief. Police looking for witnesses."

It will be so easy, Bob contemplates. He has already driven by his target so often and is sure that early in the morning when the bank opens, there aren't any customers. Those who go to work are already busy doing their jobs and the others are still sleeping at home. He can start later at his job in the kitchen firm because they've got irregular hours. When he comes in later, he goes home later. But his job is so boring. The whole day he stands in line making kitchen cabinets. If all goes well today, he will be able to take a few weeks holiday with all that money. A new car is also on his wish list. And maybe with a super Porsche he will finally get a girlfriend. He is already 19 years old and has never had a relationship with girls. They are so complicated. They want to go out and prefer a guy with a lot of money. They're not interested in a poor worker like him. He doesn't earn very much money. He's got a small apartment in a small town, where it is cheaper than living in a city.

After finishing school he got this job in the kitchen factory. You don't need to be very intelligent to stand all day on the assembly line building kitchen cabinets. He also wasn't too smart in school, either. But he didn't want to live at home anymore and now has to make sure that the money he earns lasts until the end of the month. Life can be so hard and so unfair. Most of his friends went to college and are now far away. They don't contact him anymore. He didn't have enough money to go to the university but even if he did, his grades weren't good enough. No college would have taken him, so he didn't even try to get into one.

He's a loser. But today things will change, and everything will get better. He's sure that nothing can go wrong. He will go into the bank at eight o'clock, the moment the bank clerk opens the door. Then he will show him his gun. It's not a real one, but you can't tell the difference. The pistol looks very authentic. There have already been many bank robbers who have used fake guns and the people in the bank didn't notice it. If they look real, no one wants to take a chance of being shot. And the banks are insured. Why should the bank clerk risk his life for the money that will be paid back by the insurance company?

He slowly drinks his coffee and reads the newspaper, as he does every morning. They write about everything that happens in the world. The earthquake in China was devastating. The floods in Thailand took many lives. The driver crashed into another car while recklessly passing careful drivers. Everyday there is so much bad news. And tomorrow, when the people get up and read their newspaper at breakfast, they will read about him. "Bank robber got away without a trace." Naturally, they will not know it is him. No one will find out that he is the thief. He will also hold onto the money for awhile until the air is clear so that he doesn't get exposed. It is so dumb when someone robs a bank and suddenly has a lot of money. He will play the lottery in the future and one day will be surprised with a big win. That is what he plans to tell all his friends. But he doesn't actually have any good friends.

He is single and always alone. He's feeling so lonely. His biggest wish is to finally have a loving partner. That's why he got the idea with the bank. He needs the money so he can show the girls in town that he is a good catch. The women always look at the material worth of a man and not at his character. Bob is a good, lovable man. But no one shows any interest in him because he hasn't got a penny. His old car will probably fall apart soon. Where will he get the money for a new car when it finally dies, if not from the bank?

Yes, he is sure everything will go well. He will go to work an hour later and say he didn't hear the alarm clock and slept too long. Although everything will be different after the bank robbery, he will try his best to remain normal and act like he does every other day. He looks at the clock. It's time to go.

He gets into his car and turns the key. Nothing happens. "Oh no, not today," he cries out angrily. It can't be possible that the car won't start today. If he gets to the bank too late, then customers will be there. He doesn't want to take any hostages or frighten any people he doesn't know. Deep inside he's got a big heart. He's a good person. The bank robbery is a necessity in his eyes. He hasn't got any other chance but to take some money from the bank in order to have a better life. He has no intention of hurting anyone. That's the reason he has to get there exactly at eight o'clock when the bank opens. He turns the key again and the car starts. He is relieved. Now nothing will be able to stop him from carrying out his plan.

It isn't long before he is caught on the highway in a traffic jam. "This just isn't my day," he exclaims. "This must be a bad sign for me. Maybe God is trying to keep me from doing something stupid?" The cars drive slowly further on and pass the police car, which stands behind the stalled car. Bob gets a red face as he passed them, as if they could read his mind and already know what he is planning to do today. He's got a bad conscience. He didn't do anything wrong yet but he's already getting a terrible feeling about doing something wrong.

Still, there is no way that he is going to change his mind. His plan is perfect, and he's sticking to it. It will be so easy to get some money. He needs it. The police will not arrive quickly enough to follow his car. Although they are here on the highway now and very near to the bank, he must acknowledge. Will that be dangerous for him? He contemplates about the time it would take the police car to get from here to the bank if they are still here when they get the call about the bank robbery. It could be that the traffic jam gets worse later and then they will be stuck for a long time. Actually it could be the best thing that could happen to him. He's seeing it as a positive thing now. He's lost his fear that this was a bad sign for him and is now more certain that nothing will go wrong.

He drives on slowly and takes the next exit. Now it will take him only five minutes, and he will still get there on time. Wishful thinking! Then suddenly the car in front of him crashes into the car that stopped at the red light. Bob nearly drives into the car and almost has an accident. "This can't be true," he calls out nervously. "What is wrong today? Everything seems to be against me getting to the bank on time." Maybe it is a sign that he should consider seriously. Normally when he drives to work in the morning, there aren't any complications or problems on the way. And today it seems as if everything is working against him. First his car doesn't start, after that the traffic jam and the police car are on the thruway and now the accident by the traffic light. "What will happen next?" he thinks.

But he is lucky. The two cars are able to drive and get out of the way. They drive to the shoulder of the road and exchange addresses for the insurance companies. Yes, the car costs him a lot of money. He has to pay a lot for the insurance in case of an accident like this one. Then there are the repair costs. There is constantly something else that needs to be repaired. The car is so old that it isn't worth any more repairs. The best thing would be to buy a new car. But Bob can't afford one. His money hardly lasts until the end of the month. It gets very tight. Sometimes he can hardly buy something to eat and even worse, he can't afford any cigarettes! That's a bad habit that he can't get rid of. He's tried everything to stop smoking. It costs him a lot of money, especially since they raised the prices. But you can't stop smoking "cold turkey". And actually it's not just cigarettes he's stuck on. He also drinks too much alcohol. Some people would probably call him an alcoholic.

He knows that it isn't healthy to drink so much. His liver is surely already damaged. And he is only nineteen! What do you say to that? He's such a young guy and already so unhealthy. "If everything goes well," he says to himself, "then I'll stop drinking so much." Yes, he thinks to himself, there will be a lot of changes in his life when he finally has more money. "Money can make you happy," he constantly repeats to himself. He's not sure how much money will be in the bank. But the robbery will all go smoothly. He's gone through it all so often in his head. "Put the money in the bag," he will order the bank assistant. He thought of everything. "Oh no," he calls out furiously. "I forgot the plastic bag at home. What shall I do now?"

He can't go into the bank without a bag! Where's he going to put the money? At this moment he notices the supermarket on the right and quickly drives into the entrance. He does so at the last minute and the car behind almost drives into Bob's car. Bob jumps out of the car and runs into the store. "What should I buy?" he contemplates. He hasn't got much time and he's getting nervous because it is getting late. If he gets to the bank too late, there could be some people already waiting in line. He's thirsty and decides to buy a bottle of water. That's enough. He hasn't got time to go shopping now. He only needs something so that he can get a plastic bag.

He approaches the two counters and must decide which line he should wait on to pay. There are people standing on both of them. "Inny, miny, meiny, mo, catch the tiger by the toe, if he hollers let him go, my mother said to choose this one." Using the child's rhyme, he lands on the right side. There is an old woman paying now. She opens her purse and takes out a lot of small change. Bob gets impatient. "I can't believe this. How come old people always have so much small change!" he exclaims under his breath. "Why does this always happen to me!" He would have gladly given the old lady the cash so that she could pay more quickly, but that would be ridiculous. Perhaps this is a bad sign that he should give up his plan to rob the bank. Should he see all these obstacles as warning signs that he should give up his plans for the day? Maybe it's not such a lucky day for him after all.

Finally he pays for his bottle and also a bit extra for a plastic bag, but it's worth it. Without a bag he can't take all that money out of the bank. He carries his bottle to his car and searches for his car keys in his pockets. Which pocket did he put them in? At this moment the bag slips out of his hand and falls to the ground. Bang. You can imagine what happens. The bottle breaks into pieces. The water leaks through the bag onto the ground. "I can't believe this!" he cries out. How can a person have so much bad luck! That's got to be a bad sign. Something is trying to keep him from doing something wrong, terribly wrong in the eyes of other people. He looks at his watch. It's already eight o'clock. He should be at the bank already and now he's got a small problem.

    He walks over to the garbage can in front of the store and throws the fragments of the bottle away. He has to keep the bag. It is not too good if it's wet, but it's better than none at all. He drives out of the parking lot and to the bank. Finally he's reached his destination. But the next problem occurs. He can't find a parking space. "What is wrong today!" he shouts. He just can't believe that everything seems to be going wrong. Now that he's finally here, he doesn't know where he should put his car. It's already so late! He's getting very nervous. Should he now give up everything and go to work? He must make up his mind. Will today be the beginning of a new life for him with a lot of money or will he end up at the end of the day just like every day?

At work his colleagues upset him daily. Why do they always have to be so cruel? Nobody seems to like him and he doesn't like anybody either. They're all idiots. They think they are better and more intelligent than he is. They laugh at him when he makes a small error, as if they never make any mistakes themselves. He can't talk to anyone at work, and the eight hours of silence makes him crazy. He must be a loser and now he's had enough of his sad life. He wants a change. He wants the money from the bank so that he'll finally be happy. Money makes the world go round! He knows that he will get enough money from the bank to give up his job so that he doesn't have to endure all those insults he hears daily from the others. They constantly criticize his weight. Maybe he eats too much or doesn't do enough sports. He's been trying to lose weight already for years, but it isn't easy. That's probably the reason that he doesn't have any good chances at getting a girl friend. Who wants to go out with such a fat guy? Not only is he fat, he's also poor. Another problem is his eyes. He can't see without glasses. And because he hasn't got too much money, he can't afford expensive glasses. So he must buy the cheapest possible. Everything in his life works against him.

That is why he has to follow through on his plan. Then he can say he won thousands of dollars in the lottery. Naturally he won't buy a Porsche, then that would be boastful. A Mercedes is also a good car. And when the girls see him in such an expensive car, they'll think he's got a lot of money. He'll be able to buy new glasses that make him look better than the ones he's got now. Of course if he uses the money for a long vacation, he might find a girlfriend there. Perhaps he can experience his first kiss, as he's never kissed a girl before. He definitely must rob this bank today.

There's got to be a change in his life, and nothing can stop him now.

He drives around the corner and has some luck. There he finds a free parking space. He's come so far now and will not turn back. At least he didn't forget his ski mask so that the cameras in the bank won't expose him. He must remain incognito. He'll put on the mask before he enters the bank. Then he will draw his pistol and threaten the bank clerk. He's gone through the procedure a hundred times in his head. And now it is time to put his plan into action. "Nothing can stop me now…" he sings quietly to himself. He walks quickly toward the entrance of the bank. Carefully he looks through the huge windows in order to see if someone is in the bank. Things are looking good. There is no one here yet. He looks at his watch; it is almost half past eight. Originally he wanted to be here at eight, but after all those bad incidents that happened to him this morning, he's half an hour late. But now nothing can go wrong. Nobody is in sight. He can follow his plan.

He puts on his mask, pulls out his pistol, and enters the bank. That was easy. He runs toward the bank clerk, shows him the fake pistol, and screams: "Put all the money in this bag". He hands the frightened man his plastic bag that is still totally wet from the broken water bottle. "Don't do anything wrong and no alarm and nothing will happen to you," he explains. He starts sweating in the warm ski cap. His eyes are barely free, and the sweat is dropping into his eyes. It's got to go fast, he thinks before someone comes into the bank. He doesn't want any problems in here. "Hurry up," he says to the bank clerk. "Put all the money in the bag, and no tricks."

He has to put the gun into the other hand in order to set his mask right. It's so hot in here! The man gives him the bag. Bob looks in and asks: "Is that all the money you've got. I told you no tricks or I'll get rough." "That is everything," answers the frightened clerk, who also starts sweating out of fear. Suddenly the room seems so hot for both of them.

Now he wants to get out of here as quickly as possible. Bob screams: "Now lie on the floor and count to twenty." He got this idea from a film on television. Before the petrified man can count to twenty, he is already around the corner. Outside he quickly takes off the mask and is relieved that no one is in the area. That was so easy. Go in, take the money, and run. That's how he planned it. It worked. He could already imagine the headlines in tomorrow morning's newspaper: "City Bank robbed: Thief still free."

He gets into his car and again it does not want to start. "This isn't possible. You can't desert me now. You've got to get me out of here," he says to the car as if it understands him. He turns the key again and is relieved that it finally starts. At first he has difficulty getting out of the parking space, and then something terrible happens. As he is driving away, he sees the police arriving. "How could that be possible?" he thinks.

Now he's got to step on the gas and drive as fast as he can. The police notice his suspicious behavior and follow him immediately. He drives out of the town and picks a small street through the countryside. In his rear –

view mirror he can see that the police are far behind. With a little luck he can lose them. He drives as fast as he can. It is so dangerous with all these curves in the road. He takes the next right, hoping that the police didn't see him. If everything goes well, he will get away with all that money and the police won't find him. He'll hide the money near his house. He's already prepared a good hiding place.

He drives quickly further and reaches a railroad crossing. This one only has a signal light and it is red at the moment. Bob doesn't know what to do. He has to decide quickly. Should he try to drive over the tracks before the train comes or should he wait? He looks in his rear mirror. Far behind but coming closer and closer is the police car. He panics. If they catch him now, he'll land in prison. He's got the money, and they'll have the evidence that he was the bank robber. He can already imagine the morning headlines: "Thief caught by railroad crossing." He's got to decide. What should he do? He's got to drive to the other side as fast as possible. He steps on the gas.

The next day the headlines in the morning newspaper read: "Deadly mistake – bank robber hit by approaching train while trying to escape police. Train conductor could not stop in time."

Theft at Dawn

"This looks like a good place to put up our tent, Paul. It's a lovely area," Joe smiled, checking out the beautiful sight.

"I don't know if you are allowed to camp here at the lake. Wasn't there a sign by the road, 'No Trespassing'? " replied Paul, looking very concerned and unsure.

Somehow they had ridden around enough together on Joe's motorbike, and the young men were glad to finally get off it after the four -hour ride.

"Yes, it's a beautiful area here in the woods," he agreed. "New York is such an enormous state with so many trees and different sized lakes. I love living here. But you know, practically every place of nature belongs to someone. Everywhere you read these annoying signs: 'No Trespassing'." Paul didn't want to get into any trouble with the owner or the police.

"You worry too much. Nobody is going to come around. There are so many hills, lakes, and trees in this state, that it is a sin when no one is able to enjoy what God has given to mankind," answered Joe.

He is not afraid of anything. He often takes his motorbike for long rides into the country. When you live in a big city, it is nice to get out of there now and then. The noise, the traffic, and so many people can make you nervous.

But in the country it is peaceful. You can think clearly about your life and he wants to help Paul forget his old girlfriend. She left him because she found another guy, and now he's very sad about it.

"Paul, don't worry so much about something happening out here. We are miles and miles away from any civilization. We're going to spend two nights here under the stars and enjoy our lives. Believe me, it will be a wonderful time."

But Paul was not so sure if he would be able to have a good time out here with his best friend Joe. The only thing he could think about was Mary. His heart was aching because he's still in love with her. "I just can't get her out of my mind," sighed Paul. "I'm constantly thinking about the good times I had with her, even if it only lasted for a couple of months."

"Forget Mary," Joe shouted, unpacking the tent from the back of his motorbike. "We're going to spend a lovely weekend out here in the woods; only the two of us and the bears."

"What?" Paul reacted frightened and looked toward the forest. "There are bears here? Nobody told me anything about that. No, no. I'm not going to sleep here when they've got those dangerous animals in the area!" He took his few belongings and placed them back into his bag.

Joe laughed. "That was only a joke. You should have seen the expression on your face when I mentioned the bears. Don't be afraid. I know this area well enough, and you can believe me, there aren't any bears. Maybe some foxes, or beavers."

Paul contemplated if foxes were dangerous too. But Joe laughed again as if it was another joke of his.

"Stop making me nervous or I'll go back home," Paul snapped annoyed.

But he knew, they're here with one motorbike and it belongs to Joe. So he must stay here as long as his friend wants to.

It didn't take long and the tent was set up. They made a camp fire and cooked a meal out of the can. Just like the country people used to do in the old days.

"Why didn't we bring more beer along?" Paul asked anxiously, because he wanted to drown his sorrow in alcohol.

"You know we haven't got as much room on the motorbike as you would have in a car. If you drink everything I brought along tonight, then you won't have anything left to drink tomorrow. But on the other hand, we can go shopping in the next town tomorrow morning if it isn't enough," sympathized Joe, placing the rest of the beer in the cold water for the next day. After a few beers, they got pretty tired.

"Let's go to sleep now. I'm very tired of the long trip, and you know it isn't comfortable on the bike so many hours. My back hurts." Joe stretched his arms out and yawned.

Soon he was snoring loudly, but Paul couldn't sleep. He only had thoughts about his old girlfriend, who left him for another fellow. He was so sad that it took hours until he finally fell asleep.

Nearby there were a couple of strangers, who had already been up the whole night. "I can't believe it!" shouted Frank, "how can you be so stupid?" He was very angry because it was David's job to get a good car for their night excursion into the nearby town.

It had been planned for weeks that they would break into the bank in Plainville. They waited until it got dark and were able to shut off the alarm before breaking in. The only thing that David had to do was to steal a car, so that they would not be identificd just in case someone was up in the middle of the night and saw the two burglars.

David shrugged his shoulders and looked to the ground. "I'm sorry Frank. But how was I to know how much gas this car had when I stole it? And on the way to the bank no one thought about the possibility that this car would run out of fuel. The only thing that interested us was the fact, that there was a lot of money in the bank safe."

"Yes, thanks to me, we now have a lot of money." He pointed excitedly to the bag on the back seat. "And thanks to you, we're stuck in the middle of the woods in this darkness, where you can't see a thing." Frank angrily got out of the car and placed the heavy green sport bag with the money over his right shoulder. David followed him.

"What are we going to do now?" asked David nervously; he was very frightened about being caught by the police. He did not want to land in prison again. He had already spent enough years there for his robbery of a jewelry store.

"We've got to get off the road and walk through the woods. We'll take a short cut to the next town and you can steal another car there. But one with enough fuel this time, so we can get all the way home. You know we've got a lot of miles to go." Frank was furious that his friend always made so many mistakes. Practically every time he planned something for them to earn some money, his friend did something wrong. One time, by a service station robbery, they almost got caught by the police because he drove the car into the ditch. They got to know each other in prison, after David had been caught during a jewel robbery and he got caught breaking into a shop. So they both had experience with the law.

"Do you know the area here well enough so we won't get lost in the forest? Tomorrow the police will certainly find out about the missing money and will search for us all over. And if they send their dogs out after us, we won't have much of a chance on foot." David was very nervous and insecure.

Frank, on the other hand, was always cool. "Don't worry about anything. I think we are near a lake here and then we're not too far from the next town. There we'll get another car, and before the bank director has his breakfast, we'll be home sleeping in our beds."

David looked up at the sky. The stars were vanishing one after another, and only the moonlight shone over their way through the huge forest. In the distance the sun was beginning to rise. If all goes well this time, he will never listen to Frank again and look for a decent job.

What a surprise as they neared the lake. Could that be possible? "Look over there, Frank," David exclaimed excitedly. "Do you see what I see?" He pointed to a motorbike standing near the lake next to a small tent.

"Be quiet and don't talk so loudly," whispered Frank. "Someone is probably sleeping there, and we don't want to wake him up. Do we?"

"Shhh, you're right. I'll be very quiet and get that motorbike for us. Then we won't have to walk anymore. I'm getting pretty tired," panted David.

"I'm half asleep already"; exclaimed Frank. "I didn't plan that we would be up for such a long time. It already took us so long to get into the bank through the basement of the other house." He had found out that the people next to the bank went on holiday. "And now we've already walked around a few hours in the dark through the woods because you stole the wrong car!"

David pushed the vehicle away from the tent into the woods very quietly so that they would not get caught.

"But now we've got this motorbike. So let's get away quickly," David gasped and let him sit behind him. Frank held the bag with the money between them.

As the sun was slowly rising behind the hills and the sunrays were glowing in the distance, the two desperate men drove away on the stolen motorbike. The sky's aurora was dark red, as if it was burning.

Paul was having nightmares and screamed so loudly that Joe woke up. He reached his hand over to him and whispered, "Paul, what's wrong? Are you alright?"

Paul quickly sat up and was still so shocked from his dream, that he did not know where he was. "Where am I?" he exclaimed and gently wiped the sleep from his eyes.

"We're together in my tent. Remember? We're camping by a lake. Are you okay?" asked Joe, worried about his dear friend.

Paul got up and left the tent. Outside he quickly noticed that the motorbike was gone and screamed. Joe rushed outside quickly and could not believe his eyes. "Where is my motorbike? I can't believe it. We are here in the middle of nowhere and someone came by and stole my bike! But there is nothing around for miles and miles, especially no people."

They both turned around slowly in order to check out the whole area, as far as they could see. "I can't believe this is happening to us, Joe. How the hell are we going to get back home?" Paul stammered nervously, again very upset and frightened.

Joe coolly took his mobile phone out of his jacket until he realized: "So stupid, there is no connection here in the woods. We could have called someone to pick us up. But don't you worry. We're in New York and not at the end of the world. We will walk to the next town and call my parents from there."

"What direction should we take?" breathed Paul excitedly because he wanted to get home as fast as possible. He was not as much of a camping freak as Joe. He preferred to sleep in his comfortable bed at home, safe from any kinds of animals or thieves that seem to be in the woods. Who knows what could have happened if the thieves, who stole the motorbike, were also murderers? Oh God, what an awful thought! They could have been killed while sleeping without having any knowledge of the dangers surrounding them! They could have been robbed! "We could have been killed!" he suddenly screamed, aware of how close his death may have been.

"You watch too many crime stories on television," Joe grinned, trying to calm him down. "Just because someone stole our motorbike, doesn't mean that our lives are in danger. If they had wanted to do us any harm, they had the opportunity while we were asleep. But we are still alive. And now the best thing to do is to walk to the next town before the day is over and call someone to pick us up. Do you agree with me?"

Paul nodded with his head. Suddenly he realized that because of all of his fears of being killed, he had finally stopped thinking about Mary, his old girlfriend.

"I'm so happy to still be alive. When you think, Joe, we could now be dead. It is as if we were given a second life. And I intend to use every minute of it and will forget Mary from now on. There are so many other things to live for. Don't you agree?" Paul looked relieved at Joe, hoping for some consolation.

"Yes, you are definitely right. Look at me. I don't need any women around telling me what to do. I'm free and I enjoy my life. The most important thing in life is to have a good friend. And you, Paul, are my good friend, my best friend. We're going to make it through the deepest forest and find our way home," Joe nods with his head and sounds determined. "We're strong and we're alive. Who needs a woman?"

"Right Joe," agreed Paul, "Who needs a woman."

"Are you sure this is the right way?" Paul murmured after a while. He isn't sure if Joe really knows where he is going and it seems to him that they are walking in a circle.

"Look at the sunrise," Joe explained. The sun is rising to our left, so we just have to keep walking to the right."

"Yes, it is such a beautiful sunrise today. Look at those lovely colors as they light up the dark sky. You know, nature is so beautiful and here the sunrise can be appreciated much better than in the city. Don't you think so?" Both remain quiet for a few minutes enjoying the sight as it got lighter minute by minute. "Beautiful," Joe sighed.

As they turn around to go further, they suddenly saw Joe's motorbike and two men sleeping on the ground. They looked each other in the eyes and knew exactly, what the other one was thinking. Quietly they approached the sleeping men and overwhelmed them at the same time, before they even knew what hit them. They found something to bind their hands and feet and were happy that they got their motorbike back.

"We are so lucky today," Joe exclaimed, as he gets on his bike. "Come Paul, we can drive to the next town and inform the police about the two robbers. They can't go anywhere." He looked at them and sympathized, "Don't worry. We won't leave you alone here by those dangerous bears in the area. We will send you the police before the bears get hungry."

Both men looked at each other wide-eyed. David thought Frank did not tell him anything about any dangerous animals in the woods. He was so scared, that he almost wet his pants. But Frank did not let them fool him. He knew that it wasn't the bears that they should worry about, but the police.

He tried to talk Joe out of leaving them here tied up. "Why don't you take your motorbike and your friend but let us free. We're not going to do you any harm."

"Don't listen to them," Paul hissed nervously. "You can't know what they are planning. They'll hit us over the head and leave us here."

"No, you're wrong. We wouldn't do anything like that," explained David, trying his best to get out of the situation. "We're harmless. We only steal cars and bikes. We wouldn't hurt anyone, that's not our thing."

"You can tell that to the police, when they come," Joe replied impatiently. He wanted to get away from them and let Paul take his place behind him on the motorbike. They drove off, leaving the burglars behind.

You can imagine how unhappy the two thieves are feeling now. David swears this is the last time he will ever listen to Frank. There will be no more robberies when the bears leave him alone. "Please God, let those bears be somewhere else," he prayed.

Joe and Paul, meanwhile, were on their way to the next town to tell the police about the thieves that had stolen their bike so that they could free them from their bondages. It would have been a mistake to trust them. Joe was sure that they would have overwhelmed him and Paul, who isn't as strong as he is. He felt responsible for his friend. After all, he persuaded him to go on this weekend camping trip with him. It was supposed to distract him from his heartache over Mary. He'll soon find another girlfriend, just as he always does, thinks Joe. Paul constantly gets a new girlfriend. He's such a handsome guy.

Joe is now 21 years old, one year older than Paul, and has had only one girlfriend to date. But they were together for two years, and when she left him, he was very disappointed. It's already been almost a year since they broke up.

They didn't notice that there was a police car driving behind them until it passed them. The police showed his stop sign and directed Joe to stop on the side of the road.

"We were on our way to…" Joe wanted to explain his situation but the policemen were nervous and told them to keep quiet.

"You can speak when we allow you to. We're looking for someone who broke into the City Bank last night. Let us see your driving license and identification papers," Stefan snapped as his colleague held a hand on his gun, ready to protect his partner, if one of the men on the motorbike got dangerous. They did not know if these two guys were the thieves, so just in case, they had their guns ready.

"But what's going on?" Paul looked nervously at the two policemen.

"Where are you fellows coming from?" asked John.

"We spent the night by the lake. We're from New York City and wanted to camp in the woods," explained Joe.

"And where is your camping equipment? Is it not so that you broke into the bank last night in Plainville and you thought we would not be on your tail so quickly?" Stefan looks at Joe's driving license, but Paul did not have any identification papers with him.

"No. Not at all," Paul shouts. "We were on our way to you because these two men had stolen our motorbike. We didn't rob any banks. We're honest people. Joe, tell him, about the two men that we left in the woods."

"Yes, we're the good guys. We were sleeping in our tent by the lake and when we woke up at dawn, our motorbike was gone. We walked around for a short time looking for the road and found these two guys with our bike in the woods. They were sleeping. So we overwhelmed them, tied them up and were on our way to the police to tell you about the theft. After all, we don't want them to starve or die of something else out there. This must be a misunderstanding. We aren't thieves, definitely not." Joe looks toward Paul for some help. He confirms his story. "Yeah, that is exactly what happened. Those two guys could be the thieves. We can bring you to them." Paul shows the direction they must drive with his finger and awaits an answer.

"What do you think," Stefan turns to his partner. "Does their story sound plausible?"

"Well, I suppose it would not hurt to follow them to the place where those other men are held captive. It is our duty to follow all information concerning the bank robbery. Maybe these two guys are telling the truth. And if not, we'll take them with us to the police station."

Joe and Paul were relieved and showed the two policemen the way back to where they left the two strangers in the woods. Who knows, maybe they really were the bank robbers!

The policemen were very surprised when they saw the two men tied together sitting on the ground. And it did not take long until they found the green bag with the money.

"Now what do you say here?" Stefan smiled astonished as he looked at all that money. And Joe and Paul were even more surprised to see so much money. They had not even seen that bag when they overpowered the two men. They only saw their motorbike, which they needed to get back home.

"Well, I suppose you two will get a reward from the bank for finding the bank robbers," explained the policeman. "That should be a lot of money, because there was so much stolen." "And we'll close our eyes about the fact that you camped here by the lake, even though it is forbidden. This is private property," Stefan grinned. They were happy to find the thieves so quickly.

"Actually you could have been a long distance away," he mentioned to the two bank robbers. "Why did you remain in the area so long?"

Frank was furious, then as always, everything was David's fault. "Because of this idiot here, we ran out of fuel and had to walk hours through the woods, and after we found the motorbike we couldn't find the road and drove in circles. We got so tired that we could not sit on the bike anymore. And then the owner found us sleeping in the woods. You can't have more bad luck then we had today."

David exclaimed: "At least we had enough luck not to get found by one of those grizzly bears. You know, they can be very dangerous."

The others all looked at each other and laughed. "Grizzly bears? Here in this peaceful beautiful country!" grinned Joe. I've already camped here many years and have never seen a bear yet.

The policemen looked a little surprised, since it was forbidden to camp here. Then they put the green bag with the money into the car and drove away with the thieves.

Joe and Paul returned to their tent and pulled the beer out of the water. "I can't believe that those guys robbed a bank. And did you see all that money?" Joe asked Paul while drinking out of the can. If I had so much money, I could do so many things. For example, buy me a new car or go on a long vacation. What would you do, if you had so much money?"

Paul contemplated the idea a few minutes. "I don't know. I suppose I would buy a motorbike and then we could return here next year to camp again." Both laughed.

"Too bad that we did not see that green bag lying on the floor," said Joe, dreaming about all that money.

"No," snapped Paul. "We would have been mistaken for the robbers and probably would have landed in prison if we had the money on us when the cops stopped us. It would have been our word against that of the thieves. Just like in all those crime films I have already seen. They would have locked us away."

Joe thinks about this probability. Who knows what would have happened if they were stopped with all that money.

"You're right. We are the good guys. We're honest fellows. Aren't we?" he grinned and opened a new can of beer. He searched for his sunglasses because the sun rose brightly over the hills and was beginning to blind him.

"It's going to be a nice day," Paul mentioned, opening another can of beer and putting on his sunglasses too. "Definitely, it was a good idea to go camping. I'm forgetting Mary already. Now I'm only thinking about the reward and what I will do with all that money."

Books in English.

FOLLOWING INSTINCTIVE BEHAVIOR :

BEING HUMAN = BEING CIVILIZED

http://www.amazon.com/are-human-behavioral-comparisons-ebook/dp/B006WTD1J0/ref=cm_cd_pdp?_encoding=UTF8&m=AG56TWVU5XWC2&cdPage=1&noLL=1&newContentID=Tx3GUGKZVZDU7O9#Customer Discussions

YEARNING FOR HEAVEN

Will Believers Achieve Eternal Life

http://www.neobooks.com/werk/15899-yearning-for-heaven.html

THIS IS A MAN'S WORLD - Isn't it?: I WANT TO KNOW WHAT LOVE IS

Eve Christensen (pen name)

http://www.amazon.com/THIS-IS-MANS-WORLD-Isnt-ebook/dp/B00I4F58EQ/ref=sr_1_16?ie=UTF8&qid=1394048003&sr=8-16&keywords=This+is+a+man%27s+world

USEFUL TIPS AND "LINKS" FOR YOUR FIRST VISIT TO SOUTH AFRICA - Travel Guide with Humor and Pictures - Personal Experiences in Cape Town, Garden Route, Pretoria and Kruger Park

(Easy to read)

http://www.amazon.com/USEFUL-LINKS-FIRST-VISIT-AFRICA-ebook/dp/B008MB4P6E/ref=pd_rhf_dp_p_d_5

www.irmgard-hetterich.jimdo.com